Getting To Know...

Nature's Children

WALRUS

Laima Dingwall

GROLIER
B O O K S

Facts in Brief

Classification of the Walrus

    Class: *Mammalia* (mammals)

    Order: *Pinnipedia* (pinnipeds)

    Family: *Odobenidae*

    Genus: *Rosmarus*

    Species: *Rosmarus divergens* (Pacific Walrus)

                Rosmarus rosmarus (Atlantic Walrus)

World distribution. Found all around the edges of the Arctic ice cap and in coastal areas as far south as Labrador.

Habitat. Shallow seas; ice packs; rocky coasts.

Distinctive physical characteristics. Downward-curving tusks; flippers; mustaches; thick layer of blubber under leathery skin.

Habits. Lives in herds; migrates in a regular pattern; feeds in the morning.

Diet. Primarily mollusks, supplemented by other small sea-bottom dwellers such as annelids and crustacea.

Edited by: Elizabeth Grace Zuraw
Design/Photo Editor: Nancy Norton
Photo Rights: Ivy Images

ISBN: 0-7172-8838-2

Have you ever wondered . . .

Most people can't help but smile when they
see a walrus. Maybe the walrus's comical face,
complete with a bristly mustache, is what does
it. Or maybe it's the friendly way the walrus
has of snuggling up to its neighbors on the ice.

But however amusing the walrus can be,
there's far more to this sea animal than first
meets the eye. If you could visit the Arctic
coast where the walrus lives, you'd see that
this big, funny-looking animal is truly a superb
cold-weather survivor. Let's take a closer look
at how the walrus lives.

The coarse whiskers on its muzzle are
about the only hair a walrus has.

Meet the Family

If the walrus held a family reunion for its North American relatives, who would come? Its cousins the sea lion and the seal, of course.

The walrus and its relatives belong to a group of animals called *pinnipeds,* a word that means "flipper feet." Because pinnipeds spend much of their time swimming in the ocean, *flippers*—wide flat limbs—are much more useful to them than ordinary legs would be.

Although walruses and their relatives are sea-living animals, they're not at all like fish. Fish breathe through gills and spend all of their life underwater. Walruses, on the other hand, have lungs, just as you do, and must come to the surface to breathe air. Furthermore, fish are cold-blooded, whereas walruses are warm-blooded. Animals are *cold-blooded* if they take on the temperature of the water and air around them. Warm-blooded walruses, just as you, have a body temperature that stays more or less the same all the time.

Walruses may need to come up for air periodically, but when they're in the water they're excellent swimmers and divers.

What Big Teeth You Have

It's easy to tell walruses from their relatives. They're the only ones with *tusks,* two very long pointed teeth, one at each corner of the mouth. The tusks start growing soon after a walrus is born. By the time the walrus is two years old, its tusks are 4 inches (10 centimeters) long. An adult male walrus might have tusks as long as 3 feet (1 meter), each weighing almost as much as a good-sized watermelon. Of course, you can't see all of a walrus's tusks. Parts of them are hidden inside its mouth.

A female walrus's tusks are shorter, narrower, and more curved than a male's.

Male tusks

Female tusks

The size of a male's tusks is important. In any argument with other males, the animal with the longest tusks usually gets his way.

9

All-purpose Tusks

In addition to its tusks, the walrus has 16 other teeth, all of which are quite small. Why are its tusks so large? Because they have several uses.

Male walruses use their tusks when they have to fight other males to show their strength. And walruses use their tusks in self-defense. Because tusks are strong and almost impossible to break, they make fierce weapons. Walruses use them to defend themselves against the Polar Bear and Killer Whale, two of their most dangerous predators. A *predator* is an animal that hunts other animals for food.

Tusks also make handy grappling hooks when a walrus wants to climb out of the water onto a slippery ice floe. The walrus simply stabs its tusks into the ice and hoists itself over the edge. Tusks are helpful for getting around on land, too. The walrus uses its tusks like ski poles, sticking them into the ice or snow and pulling itself along. Or sometimes a walrus uses its tusks just to prop its head up!

A walrus can use its tusks the way a mountain climber uses a pick. Scientists once believed that the walrus used its tusks to dig for food, but that theory has been disproved.

Walruses East and West

Two kinds of walruses live in North America: the Pacific Walrus and the Atlantic Walrus.

The Pacific Walrus lives on the western edge of the Arctic Ocean, near Alaska. The Atlantic Walrus makes its home on the eastern edge of the Arctic Ocean, near Hudson Bay and Labrador.

Opposite page: Walruses spend a good deal of time out of the water, resting and sunbathing on ice floes and beaches.

Where walruses live in North America

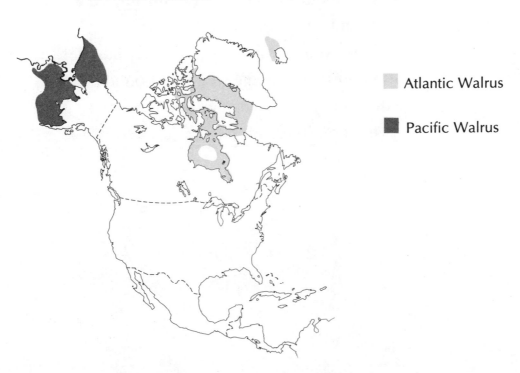

Atlantic Walrus

Pacific Walrus

As Big as a...Walrus!

The French explorer Jacques Cartier saw walruses on his early voyages to North America. When he later wrote about them, he called them "great beasts...like large oxen."

No wonder he said that. The walrus is HUGE. A full-grown male Pacific Walrus weighs 2,400 pounds (1,100 kilograms) or more. And from the tips of its whiskers to the end of its tail, it might be as long as 13 feet (4 meters). In other words, a walrus can weigh about as much as 14 full-grown adult men and be as long as a large car!

The Atlantic Walrus is slightly smaller. It weighs an average of 2,000 pounds (900 kilograms) and measures about 10 feet (3 meters) long.

A walrus's considerable bulk is covered by wrinkled skin that's up to 2 inches (about 5 centimeters) thick. The skin normally has many lumps, folds, creases, and small bumps.

Walruses Love Water

Everything about the walrus is suited to life in the water. Doesn't even the shape of the walrus's body remind you of an oversized fish? That streamlined form helps the walrus cut through the water easily and quickly.

You could be excused for not noticing the walrus's ears. They're small slits on the sides of its head. When the walrus dives underwater, a flap of skin automatically closes over each ear to keep out water. And the walrus doesn't need to worry about getting water up its nose either. A fold of skin covers its nostrils when it dives, just like built-in nose plugs.

Today's water-loving walruses trace their ancestry to bear-like creatures that existed as far back as 20 million years ago.

Cold-water Comfort

You might find swimming in cold Arctic water a chilling experience. Not the walrus. Its tough leathery skin covers a layer—up to 6 inches (15 centimeters) thick—of special fat called *blubber*. Blubber is like a snugly parka for the walrus. It keeps the walrus warm not only in icy water but also in chilly air.

The walrus's large, flat head is particularly useful when it's swimming under the ice. If the walrus needs to come to the surface for a breath of air, it uses its head as a battering ram to make a hole in the ice. You might say "Ouch!" but the walrus's sturdy head isn't hurt by such an impact.

The walrus rests at sea in a vertical position. Two inflatable air sacs, or pouches, in its neck keep its bulky head above water.

Walrus Underwater

The walrus has two pairs of flippers—one near the front of its body and another pair in the back. Its front flippers have fine long "fingers" joined by webs of skin. When the walrus spreads these fingers, the flippers become wide, powerful paddles with lots of swimming power.

The walrus uses its rear flippers like the rudder on a boat. They help the walrus change directions when it's in the water.

Walrus flipper

A walrus's layer of blubber not only keeps it warm, it helps the animal float.

Dive, Dive, Dive

The walrus dives underwater to find food and to escape predators. It usually finds its food in shallow water close to shore, but it can dive as deep as 300 feet (91 meters). And it can stay underwater for as long as 15 minutes without coming up for air!

How does the walrus do it? After all, walruses don't breathe through gills as fish do. They have lungs, so they need air.

When a walrus is underwater, its muscles relax and its heart rate slows down. That way it uses up the supply of air in its lungs slowly. This allows the walrus to stay underwater for a long time.

The walrus is a very graceful swimmer— and a fast one. It can reach speeds of up to 15 miles (24 kilometers) per hour in the water. That's about five times the speed of the fastest human swimmer!

Because walruses feed at the bottom of bodies of water, they prefer shallow areas less than 60 feet (18 meters) deep.

Walruses sometimes lie about in shallow water and wait for the incoming tide to lift them up onto a rocky ledge.

Thump, Thump, Thump

The walrus may be graceful in the water, but on land—that's a different story. There it bumps along like an overgrown caterpillar.

The walrus uses its short, but very sturdy, flippers to push itself along the ground. It can swing its back flippers forward and fan them out to brace itself. This way, the walrus can push itself up and forward with a lunging thump. And if a walrus is on an ice flow and in a hurry, it hooks its tusks into the ice and pulls itself forward.

The walrus may look clumsy and comical as it waddles and thumps along, but it can reach surprising speeds when it's pursuing an intruder or escaping danger.

Ask a Walrus to Dinner

Opposite page: *A sensitive mustache and muzzle are the walrus's main tools in its search for food.*

A walrus will eat almost any small creatures it can find on the sea bottom. It often eats shrimps, whelks, marine worms, and sea cucumbers. But its favorite food, and the mainstay of its diet, is clams.

How does a walrus find clams in the sand on the ocean's bottom? Scientists once believed that the walrus raked along the bottom with its tusks to pry clams loose. Now researchers have evidence that a walrus uses only its bristly mustache.

A walrus's mustache is made up of some 400 very stiff, thick, strong hairs arranged in neat rows. Each hair is tipped with sensitive nerves. That kind of mustache is like having 400 extra fingers to help you find food!

The walrus is a very delicate eater. It can eat clams without swallowing any part of the shell. No one has ever figured out how it can do this. Somehow the walrus just sucks the soft clam meat right out of the shell, using its tongue and thick, rubbery lips.

Wall-to-Wall Walrus

After a good feed, a walrus usually likes to haul itself out of the water to rest or snooze in the sun. A group of walruses often has its own favorite *oogli*. That's the name that the *Inuit,* or Eskimo peoples, have given to the place where walruses gather. An oogli can be a rocky beach or nothing more than a large ice floe surrounded by deep water.

No matter what or where the oogli is, one thing is sure. The oogli is always crowded with walruses. In fact, sometimes so many walruses snuggle so closely together that it's hard to tell where one walrus ends and another begins. Together they look like one giant walrus carpet!

Walruses like being with each other, and often haul out in huge groups on ice floes or rocky islands.

Warring Walruses

With so many walruses gathered together on the same oogli, it's not surprising that clashes occur. At times, walruses fight so loudly that their calls can be heard 1.5 miles (2 kilometers) away!

What do walruses fight about? Perhaps one walrus has rolled over and accidentally jabbed another one with its tusks. Or a walrus might fancy sleeping in another walrus's cozy spot.

Sometimes serious confrontations take place. Two walruses will face one another, rear up on their flippers, and throw their heads back to threaten each other with their tusks. But such fights rarely come to blows. The walrus with the shorter tusks usually gives way. Soon all the walruses relax and lie quietly together again—until the next squabble.

Tusks are important in settling walrus confrontations.
The animal with the longest tusks usually gets its way.

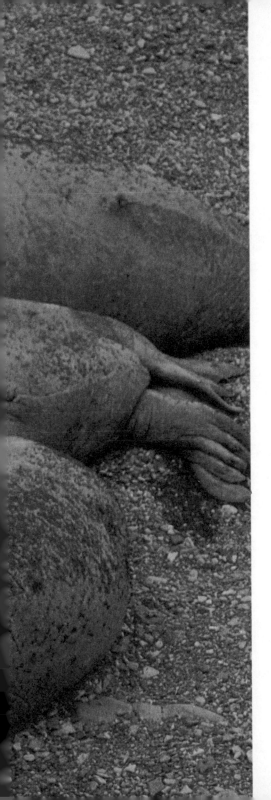

In the Pink

When a walrus hauls itself out of the water onto an oogli, its thick, leathery skin is quite pale and gray. But after the animal has stretched out in the sun for a few minutes, its skin slowly turns a rosy shade of pink.

No, the walrus isn't getting sunburned! It's just that the blood vessels under the animal's skin expand in the warm sun. Blood rushes into the vessels, giving the walrus's skin a rosy color. While the walrus was down in the icy water, its blood flowed deep into its body to support its internal organs. As the blood flowed away from the walrus's body surface, the animal's skin lost its rosy color and turned gray.

It's not magic! Cozily on land after a chilly swim, the walrus's skin changes from dull gray to rosy pink.

33

The More the Merrier

A lone walrus is a sad walrus. Walruses are very social animals and love nothing more than the company of their own kind.

Walruses live and travel in groups. There might be a hundred or more walruses in a group, all mixed together, old and young, male and female. Female walruses are called *cows,* and the males are *bulls.* If you guessed that a young walrus is called a *calf,* you're right. During *mating season,* the time of year during which animals come together to produce young, the older bulls drive away the younger ones. The young males sometimes form their own groups and stay on the edge of the main group.

Walruses sometimes form herds of up to 2,000 bulls, cows, and calves.

Walrus on the Move

A walrus spends the summer months in the waters along the edge of the Arctic ice. The Pacific Walrus summers along the northern coasts of Siberia and Alaska. Its Atlantic cousin spends summers on the edge of the Atlantic Arctic.

Come winter, when the northernmost seas start to freeze over, both the Pacific and Atlantic Walruses travel south. They *migrate*, or travel, to places where the warmer currents and shallower waters keep the ice from closing up the bays and the sea. Sometimes they might do a little ice-hitchhiking. If the big ice floes are heading in the right direction, the walruses drift along with them.

Once spring rolls around, the walrus travels north again.

When migrating, walruses like to hitch a ride on ice. But if the ice floe heads off in the wrong direction, it's time for the walruses to start swimming!

Mating Time

Opposite page:
A female walrus is ready to start a family at about 6 or 7 years of age. Males don't fully mature until they're about 15 years old.

After their springtime migration to the far north, it's time for the walruses to mate. First, each male walrus stakes out a territory on an ice floe. A *territory* is an area that an animal lives in and defends from other animals of the same kind.

A male walrus mates with as many as 30 females in a season. A female walrus, however, usually mates with only one male. All the females that the male has mated with crowd into the territory he has claimed. He guards these females and fights off any other bulls that try to come near.

Once mating season is over, the bulls no longer are concerned about their territories or about the other males. In fact, they don't even worry about the females that they have just been so fiercely protecting. The females have to raise their young with no help from the fathers.

Walrus Birthday Time

About a year after mating, a female walrus is ready to give birth. If possible, she uses an ice floe near the oogli as her nursery. Usually only one baby is born. Twins are very rare. At birth, a baby walrus is tiny—at least by walrus standards. The newborn weighs from 100 to 150 pounds (45 to 68 kilograms). That's about as heavy as most full-grown women!

A newborn walrus is weak and helpless. Its layer of blubber is very thin, and it has a coat of only short, silvery gray baby hair to protect it from the cold. It's not surprising that walrus babies spend much of their time trying to keep warm by cuddling close to their mothers.

As a baby walrus snuggles next to its mother, it *nurses* often—it drinks the thick, creamy milk in its mother's body. The young walrus will drink this rich milk until it's almost 2 years old.

Opposite page:
A walrus mother and baby are seldom apart, whether on ice or land or in the water. When the mother dives for food, she often clasps the calf in her flippers and takes it along.

A calf stays with its mother and nurses until it's two years old. By then it's able to find food by itself.

Walrus Motherhood

The female walrus is an excellent mother. In fact, she'll sometimes even adopt an orphaned baby walrus and raise it as her own.

The mother walrus and her baby are very affectionate. They spend much of their time giving each other tiny "kisses" by rubbing their bristly mustaches. They even give each other walrus hugs, and the mother sometimes holds her baby with her flippers.

A mother walrus tries never to let her baby wander out of her sight. If a baby should get separated from its mother, it cries so loudly that she'll soon come to the rescue.

A young walrus can swim soon after it's born. Often it swims side by side with its mother, but sometimes it has a hard time keeping up. When that happens, the baby climbs onto its mother's back and holds her sides tightly with its flippers. Sometimes it will hitchhike a ride this way for hours.

Overleaf:
It's easy to see: With skin up to 2 inches (about 5 centimeters) thick, and about a 6-inch (15-centimeter) layer of blubber, the stout walrus is built for life in the icy Arctic.

Time To Leave Mother

A young walrus is usually safe as long as its mother is nearby. She protects it and teaches it how to find its own food and how to avoid Polar Bears, Killer Whales, and other enemies of young walruses. After two years, it's time for the mother to give birth to a new baby and for the young walrus to make a life of its own.

The young walrus sunning itself on the oogli probably has a long happy life ahead of it. It can go clam-digging, enjoy cold-water swims, and snuggle with other walruses for many years to come. Some walruses live for as long as 40 years.

Words To Know

Blood Vessels   Tubes, arteries, and veins through which blood flows in the body.

Blubber   A layer of fat on an animal's body that keeps the cold out and body heat in.

Bull   A male walrus.

Calf   A baby walrus.

Cold-blooded   Having a body temperature that's controlled by the temperature of the surrounding air or water.

Cow   A female walrus.

Flippers   Wide flat limbs adapted specially for swimming.

Inuit   The Eskimo peoples of North America.

Lungs   Parts of the body that take in air and put it into the blood.

Mate   To come together to produce young.

Migration   A seasonal journey to find food, a suitable climate to live, or a place to mate and bear young.

Nurse   To drink milk from a mother's body.

Oogli   The Inuit word for a walrus gathering place.

Pinnipeds   A group of animals that have flippers.

Predator   An animal that hunts other animals for food.

Sac   A pouch-like structure.

Territory   The area that an animal or group of animals lives in and often defends from other animals of the same kind.

Tusks   Two elongated, pointed teeth that extend outside the walrus's mouth.

Index

PHOTO CREDITS
Cover: Stephen J. Krasemann, *Valan Photos.* **Interiors:** Leonard Lee Rue III, 4, 19. */Thomas Stack & Associates:* Thomas Kitchin, 7. */Valan Photos:* Stephen J. Krasemann, 8, 12, 17, 27, 28, 35, 36. / Wayne Lynch, 11, 23, 39. */Visuals Unlimited:* Tom J. Ulrich, 15. */Canada In Stock/Ivy Images:* H. Kiliaan, 24; Gary Crandall, 31. */Fred Bruemmer, 21, 32-33, 40, 42, 44-45.

Getting To Know...

Nature's Children

HAWKS

Merebeth Switzer

GROLIER
B O O K S

Facts in Brief

Classification of North American hawks

Class: *Aves* (birds)

Order: *Falconiformes* (falcon-shaped birds)

Family: *Accipitridae* (hawk family)

Genus: 5 North American genera (accipiters, buteos, falcons, harriers, and osprey)

Species: 17 North American species

World distribution.   Found throughout the world.

Habitat.   Varies with species; family ranges over most kinds of territory.

Distinctive physical characteristics.   Dark back with lighter underside; three sets of eyelids; hooked beak and strong talons.

Habits.   Active during the day; eats prey whole.

Diet.   Birds and small mammals; varies with species.

Edited by: Elizabeth Grace Zuraw
Design/Photo Editor: Nancy Norton
Photo Rights: Ivy Images

Have you ever wondered . . .

Has anyone ever said to you, "You have eyes like a hawk?" If they have, what they mean is that you have very sharp eyesight. But no matter how good your eyesight is, it can't match a hawk's. As these amazing birds fly overhead, they can spot the slightest movement in the grass beneath them. Their eyesight is eight to ten times more powerful than people's!

Good eyesight is important for a hawk. It lives by hunting. It hunts as it flies or from its perch high up in a tree, so it has to be able to spot a likely meal from quite a distance. But excellent eyesight is just one of the many interesting things about the hawk. Let's find out more about this incredibly sharp-eyed bird.

Hawks are found almost everywhere in the world. The kind of hawk shown here—the Swainson's Hawk—lives in the western United States.

The First Flight

The young hawk stands at the edge of its nest high in a tree and looks down. It's a long way to the ground. In the nest, its brothers and sisters are flapping their wings, as if to say, "My turn next."

Then suddenly, as the young hawk is just about to launch itself out of the nest, it's pushed from behind by an over-eager sister. Down it goes, fluttering and flapping. It lands safely with a gentle thump, its eyes gleaming brightly. It has *fledged,* made its first flight! Now the youngster is ready to take its place in the wonderful world of hawks.

These Red-shouldered Hawk chicks will soon be taking their first leap into flight.

Hawks Everywhere

There is a type of hawk for every kind of habitat in North America. A *habitat* is a type of place an animal lives in. In fact, hawks are found almost everywhere in the world except in Antarctica. They live almost anywhere they can find food. Some types of hawks prefer forests; others, grasslands; and still others, semi-desert areas.

Some hawks have two homes—a summer home, where they nest, and a winter home. Why? These hawks nest in regions where the winters are cold and many animals *hibernate,* or go into a kind of deep sleep in the winter. Hawks don't hibernate. To find enough food in winter, they must *migrate,* or fly, south to warmer climates.

The Northern Goshawk, which lives in the far north, is rarely seen.

The Hawk Family

If you had to draw a family tree of North American hawks, it would have five main branches. Each branch would stand for one of the five different kinds of hawks: accipiters (ax-IP-uh-ters), buteos (BYOO-tee-ohs), falcons (FAL-cuns), harriers (HARRY-ers), and ospreys (AH-sprees). Some of these main branches would sprout smaller branches. The buteo branch would have more smaller branches than any other hawks because there are 13 kinds of buteos in North America. The osprey and harrier branches, on the other hand, would have no smaller branches.

You can recognize the different hawks by the size and shape of their wings and tails.

accipiter

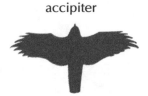

The shorter, more rounded wings of the accipiters are ideal for hunting in densely forested areas.

buteo

The buteos are great soarers, thanks to their broad wings and fan-like tails.

falcon

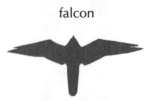

With their narrow pointed wings and tapered tails, falcons are built for speed.

harrier

The long rounded wings and lengthy tail of the harrier make it a very agile hunter.

osprey

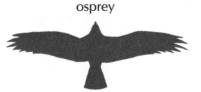

The long narrow wings of the osprey appear bowed, much like a gull's.

An osprey guards its nest. Ospreys sometimes are called "fish hawks" because of their skill at catching fish.

11

Mini Hawks and Maxi Hawks

You probably think of hawks as quite large birds and, indeed, some of them are. The osprey, for instance, can reach a length of 25 inches (65 centimeters) and has a wingspan of more than 65 inches (165 centimeters). The kestrel, on the other hand, is smaller than a robin. This mini falcon is little more than 8 inches (20 centimeters) long!

Generally speaking, hawks aren't very colorful birds. They come mainly in shades of bluish gray or brown. Their backs are usually quite dark. Their underparts are lighter, often marked with bars and speckles. A few hawks, however, have some brighter-colored feathers here and there. Red-tailed Hawks are even named for the splashes of color in their *plumage,* or covering of feathers.

Unlike many birds, male and female hawks don't look very different from each other. The color of their feathers and their markings are usually the same. But you might be able to tell which is which if you saw them together. The female is slightly larger than the male.

Opposite page: Few hawks are as colorful—or as small—as the American Kestrel.

13

Acrobats of the Air

*Opposite page:
The Rough-
legged Hawk
belongs to the
buteo branch of
the hawk family.*

Each kind of hawk has its own special flying skills. Some are able to *soar,* or rise high on air currents, and glide for great distances without flapping their wings. Others must flap hard to fly, but are masters of fast stops and quick turns. And still others can hover above the ground like miniature helicopters. Such maneuvers allow them to check out intended prey before diving down from the sky after it. *Prey* is an animal hunted by another animal for food.

How Hawks Soar
When the sun warms the air closest to the ground, that air begins to rise in the shape of a bubble. While rising, the bubble of warm air draws in the surrounding cooler air. The result is a rising column of warm air that, as it climbs, forms a thermal, *a swirling doughnut-shaped mass at the top. Once a hawk detects and gets inside a thermal, it can glide effortlessly and, at the same time, be lifted higher and higher.*

Champion Sky Diver

Imagine diving through the air at 180 miles (290 kilometers) per hour. That's faster than many race cars go! But believe it or not, that's exactly how fast one kind of hawk, the Peregrine Falcon, can dive after its prey.

Hawks that do a lot of fast diving have developed a special way to protect their nostrils from the sudden rush of air as they dive. A system of plugs helps to close off their nostrils and control the amount of air that is taken into their lungs.

The Red-tailed Hawk is the most common hawk found in North America. It soars in high, wide circles, but once it spots prey below, it descends quickly on the prey.

Super Sight

Few birds can judge distances as accurately as a hawk. That's because other birds don't need to—their food stays put. A hawk's meal, however, is often on the move. And if the hawk is to catch a moving dinner, it must know where to pounce. A hawk's eyes, like those of many other animal hunters, are in the front of its head, rather than at the sides or top. This helps the hawk judge distances accurately.

Because the hawk also has very good eyesight, when it flies over a field it can see a mouse in the grass far below. With such super eyesight, the hawk has little need for a good sense of smell or for extremely sharp hearing. A hawk may use these other senses, but its nose and ears are probably not much more highly developed than yours.

Like all hawks, a Swainson's Hawk has sharp eyes that don't miss much.

Eye Protection

Hawks depend on their eyes for survival. Without good eyesight they couldn't hunt and would starve quickly. Because hawks can't just go to the store and buy a pair of glasses if they have eye problems, they have to protect their eyes. They do so by having three sets of eyelids.

The upper and lower eyelids of hawks look much like yours. The difference is that hawks move the lower lids up over their eyes when they blink. The third eyelid moves from side to side across the eye, rather like a windshield wiper, to help clean and moisten the eye's surface.

Buteos such as this Red-tailed Hawk do most of their hunting as they circle high over open fields. Even when they pause to rest, however, they keep a sharp eye out in case an easy meal happens by.

Winged Hunters

People have favorite foods—and so do hawks. Some kinds of hawks snap up grasshoppers, butterflies, and other insects. Other hawks prefer snakes, birds, rabbits, or mice. And one kind of hawk, the osprey, dines mainly on fish. Whatever their choice of food, all hawks have one thing in common. They all hunt during the daytime—unlike owls that hunt mostly at night.

Hawks hunt with remarkable skill, taking mostly the sick or unskilled members of their prey. By removing the weak, they help maintain the balance of nature and ensure the survival of the healthiest animals.

The Red-shouldered Hawk is found in the eastern and central regions of the United States, as well as in California.

Blending In

Although hawks are skilled hunters, their different prey are skilled at escaping capture. The hawk must, therefore, sneak up quickly on its prey without alarming it. For this purpose, the hawk's coloring is very useful. As a hawk flies overhead, its light underbelly helps it to blend in with the sky so that it isn't easily seen by animals on the ground.

Hawks that hunt by perching in trees and watching for movement can also be difficult for land animals to see. By sitting very still, hawks blend in with the sky from one direction, while their dark backs and shoulders give the appearance of a broken branch when viewed from behind. *Camouflage* is the name given to the coloring and markings on an animal that blend in with its surroundings.

In a casual glance from a distance, you might completely miss this Sharp-shinned Hawk as it blends in with the beiges and grays of a tree's trunk.

Hunting Tactics

If you've ever seen a hawk flying overhead, you've probably seen a hunter at work. Many hawks watch for movement on the ground as they fly. If they see a small animal scurrying through the grass, they dive down and grab it with their sharp claws. The osprey uses much the same technique when hunting for fish.

Some kinds of hawks sit motionless in trees waiting for unsuspecting animals to pass by. Then, whooosh!—they pounce on their prey.

Hawks that hunt other birds for food use another tactic. They dive after their flying dinner and snatch it right in midair!

Hawks are known as *birds of prey* because they hunt other animals. Hawks are especially suited for hunting because of excellent eyesight to spot prey, powerful claws to catch it, and sharp hooked beaks to tear the prey's flesh. Birds of prey are also called *raptors.*

Hawks don't sing as other birds do, but when disturbed, they will produce piercing whistles and screams or loud chattering sounds.

26

Talons and Toes

Like the skilled hands of a baseball player catching a ball, the hawk's feet work to grab hold of its prey. Each foot has four strong toes with sharp claws called *talons*. Three toes point forward, while the fourth points to the back. This back toe helps in gripping— much like your thumb does when you grab something.

The hawk's strong toes serve another useful purpose as well. Their firm grip enables the hawk to sleep on its perch without any danger of falling off.

A hawk's talons

Your chances are fairly good for spotting a Red-tailed Hawk. These birds often perch on the branches of dead trees or on tall poles, making them easy to see.

A Meat-eating Beak

All birds have beaks that help them eat their food, and the hawk is no exception. Its powerful curved beak enables it to tear larger prey into smaller chunks that it can swallow.

A hawk usually eats every morsel of its catch—including fur, feathers, feet, and even bones. Then its stomach goes to work sorting out food from garbage. The bits that the hawk cannot digest are formed into small round pellets that the bird later spits up.

The Northern Goshawk, an accipiter, prefers to live in woodland areas. This hawk hunts rabbits and large birds.

A Ballet of Love

Hawks take only one mate each *mating season,* the time of year during which animals come together to produce young. Some hawks even mate for life. The male and female meet during the early spring. Before mating, many hawk pairs perform a remarkable aerial ballet as part of their *courtship*, the process of attracting a mate. The hawks dart and swoop toward each other and may even clasp each other's feet in midair for a few seconds. Then they swoop off and back together again. Sometimes this ballet is repeated at other times of the year by a pair of hawks who just seem to be enjoying the freedom of flying.

A pair of Red-shouldered Hawks rest on a plant in a southern cypress swamp.

Nesting

Most kinds of hawks build isolated nests high up in trees or on the sides of cliffs. And in recent years, some cliff-dwelling hawks have even taken to building their homes on the tops of high-rise buildings! Cities are busy places, but high above the streets, no one bothers the hawks. And in cities there are plenty of pigeons to provide a good and steady supply of food for a young family of *chicks,* as hawk babies are called.

Hawks that live on the prairies or in marshy areas, where trees are scarce, build their nests on the ground. These hawks are skillful in hiding their nests in the grass or in a tangle of marsh plants.

The ground-nesting Northern Harrier hides its nest well in tall marsh grasses.

There are as many different kinds of nests as there are hawks. Some hawks are content to borrow nests no longer used by crows or other birds, but many build their own. Often a male and female build their nest together very early in the spring. They make use of twigs, branches, dried leaves, or any other materials they can find.

Some hawks make sturdy nests, which they add to from year to year. On the other hand, if a safe enough place is available—a cliff, perhaps, or rocky hillside that few enemies can get to—a hawk may not bother with a nest at all. The mother will simply lay her eggs on the bare ground.

On a rocky ledge, a Prairie Falcon and its babies are safely out of sight from above and below.

The Long, Cold Wait

The female lays her eggs early in the spring. In northern areas you can sometimes see a mother hawk covered with snow as she huddles over her eggs to protect them and keep them warm.

The female has a special way of keeping her eggs warm even in the coldest weather. As she gets ready to lay her eggs, some of her breast feathers fall out and she lines her nest with them. The bare patch left on her breast is supplied with extra blood. As she settles down on her eggs, this bare patch supplies added warmth to the eggs.

Most hawks lay two to five eggs that take about a month to *hatch,* or produce a baby. The female usually lays one egg every other day, but she begins sitting on them the very first day. This means that each egg hatches on a different day.

These Northern Harrier chicks await the hatching of the remaining two eggs in their nest.

Thieves Beware

Although hawks are very secretive about their nests, it's usually easy to tell when a nest is near by the uproar most hawk parents make at the slightest approach of an intruder. They screech and scream, trying to scare away the intruder—and usually they succeed. But if a determined egg-or chick-snatcher persists, the parents defend their nest ferociously, attacking with sharp talons and beaks. A thief lucky enough to escape these protective parents won't soon forget their message: "Leave us alone, or else!"

Like all hawk parents, this pair of Red-tailed Hawks is highly protective of its new family.

Out of the Eggs

For the first week of its life, a baby hawk is quite helpless, barely able to lift its head. It's covered in soft *down,* or very soft feathers, and its eyes are large and dark.

The parents feed their babies tiny pieces of meat, and shelter them day and night with their bodies. At the first sign of rain the female crouches over her *nestlings*—birds too young to leave their nest—to protect them.

In the second week of a young hawk's life, remarkable changes begin to take place. The little hawk has learned to hold its head up, and it starts demanding food with loud, piercing squeals. Sometimes the babies become quite pushy and grab a piece of meat that's too big for them. Their watchful parent patiently helps tear the meat into smaller pieces.

The young hawks grow with amazing speed, and they need plenty of food to do this. Imagine eating your own body weight in food every day! That's what some baby hawks need. Finding enough food for this hungry family keeps the hawk parents very busy.

Opposite page: *A hawk parent feeds its chick. Young hawks remain in the nest anywhere from four to eight weeks.*

Flying and Hunting Practice

By the end of their first month, the young birds are ready to try flying. Usually the first flight is a short glide from their nest tree to some nearby branch. It'll take some time for the youngsters to master the skills of flying and match the acrobatics of their parents. But they're eager to practice their new skill.

As the young hawks become comfortable in the air, they begin to hunt for themselves. By early summer they're ready to leave the nest and go off on their own.

A hawk chick makes some bumpy landings in its early attempts to fly.

On Their Own

The first year of a young hawk's life is a difficult one. The hawk must find enough food for itself and it has to fight off predators who can recognize a young inexperienced bird. And if the young hawk has to go south for the winter, it must undertake a long and exhausting flight on its own.

Yet in spite of the dangers, hawks are clever birds whose will to survive is strong. If they learn their survival lessons well, they'll have several families of their own and will live for as long as 10 years.

Words To Know

Bird of prey   A bird that hunts other animals for food.

Camouflage   The coloring and markings on an animal that blend in with its surroundings.

Chick   A baby bird.

Courtship   The process of attracting a mate.

Down   Very soft feathers.

Fledge   To make a first flight.

Habitat   The area or type of area in which an animal or plant naturally lives.

Hatch   To break out of an egg.

Hibernate   To fall into a kind of heavy sleep during the winter. When animals hibernate, their breathing and heart rates slow, and their body temperature goes down.

Mating season   The time of year during which animals come together to produce young.

Migrate   To travel from one place to another, usually in search of food, a suitable climate to live, or a place to mate and raise young.

Nestling   A bird that is too young to leave the nest.

Plumage   The covering of feathers on a bird.

Predator   An animal that hunts other animals for food.

Prey   An animal hunted by other animals for food.

Raptor   Another name for a bird of prey.

Soar   To rise higher into the air on air currents, using little or no wing movement.

Talons   The claws of a hawk or other bird of prey.

Index

PHOTO CREDITS
Cover: Thomas Kitchin, *Valan Photos.* **Interiors:** *Valan Photos:* Wilf Schurig, 4; Albert Kuhnigk, 15, 27, 44; Thomas Kitchin, 36. /Maslowski Photo, 7. /Dr. George K. Peck, 9, 28, 39. /Tim Fitzharris, 10, 20. /*Visuals Unlimited:* Joe McDonald, 12. /*Ivy Images:* Alan & Sandy Carey, 16, 31. /Bill Ivy, 19. /National Museum of Natural Science, 23. /Vince Claerhout, 24. /*Thomas Stack & Associates:* John Shaw, 32. /Mark Peck, 35. /Barry Ranford, 40-41. /James Richards, 42.